# A SLEEP OF PRISONERS

CHRISTOPHER FRY

# A SLEEP OF PRISONERS

*A Play*

*Geoffrey Cumberlege*
OXFORD UNIVERSITY PRESS
LONDON    NEW YORK    TORONTO
1951

*Oxford University Press, Amen House, London E.C. 4*

GLASGOW NEW YORK TORONTO MELBOURNE WELLINGTON
BOMBAY CALCUTTA MADRAS CAPE TOWN

*Geoffrey Cumberlege, Publisher to the University*

? *Worth* 1932

PRINTED IN GREAT BRITAIN

*To*

ROBERT GITTINGS

*Dear Robert*

*It is nineteen years this summer since you persuaded me to take a holiday from my full-time failure to make a living, and sat me down, with a typewriter and a barrel of beer, in the empty rectory at Thorn St. Margaret. I had written almost nothing for five or six years, and I was to write almost nothing again for five years following, but the two months we spent at Thorn, two months (it seems to me now) of continuous blazing sunshine, increased in me the hope that one day the words would come. It was all very well that I should look obstinately forward to plays which I showed no sign of writing. It was an extraordinary faith which made you also look obstinately forward to them. The ten years in which you loyally thought of me as a writer when clearly I wasn't, your lectures to me on my self-defensive mockery of artists, and those two leisure months under the Quantocks, were things of friendship which kept me in a proper mind.*

*We were talking even then, as we are talking, with greater instancy, now, of the likelihood of war. And I think we realized then, as we certainly now believe, that progress is the growth of vision: the increased perception of what makes for life and what makes for death. I have tried, as you know, not altogether successfully, to find a way for comedy to say something of this, since comedy is an essential part of men's understanding. In* A Sleep of Prisoners *I have tried to make a more simple statement, though in a complicated design where each of four men is seen through the sleeping thoughts of the others, and each, in his own dream, speaks as at heart he is, not as he believes himself to be. In the later part of Corporal Adams' dream the dream changes to a state of thought entered into by all the sleeping men, as though, sharing their prison life, they shared, for a few moments of the night, their sleeping life also.*

C.

## A SLEEP OF PRISONERS

*First performed in Oxford at the University Church on 23 April 1951 and in London at St. Thomas's Church, Regent Street, on 15 May 1951 with the following cast:*

| | |
|---|---|
| Private David King | LEONARD WHITE |
| Private Peter Able | DENHOLM ELLIOTT |
| Private Tim Meadows | HUGH PRYSE |
| Corporal Joe Adams | STANLEY BAKER |

*The play was produced by* Michael MacOwan

# CHARACTERS

PRIVATE DAVID KING

PRIVATE PETER ABLE

PRIVATE TIM MEADOWS

CORPORAL JOE ADAMS

*The interior of a church, turned into a prison camp. One prisoner,*
PETER ABLE, *is in the organ loft, playing 'Now the day is over'*
*with one finger. Another,* DAVID KING, *is looking at the memorial*
*tablets on the wall. Four double bunks stand between the choir-*
*stalls. A pile of straw and a pile of empty paillasses are on the*
*chancel steps.*

DAVID [*shouting up to the organ loft*]. Hey, Pete, come down and
tell me what this Latin
Says. If it's Latin.

PETER [*still playing*]. Why, what for?

DAVID. For the sake of that organ. And because I want to know
If 'Hic jacet' means what it looks like.

[PETER *changes the tune to 'Three Blind Mice'.*
[*In a flash of temper.*]
And because I said so, that's what for, because
I said so! And because you're driving me potty.

PETER. Excuse me a minute: this is the difficult bit.

DAVID. If you want it difficult, go on playing. I swear
I'll come up there and put my foot through you.

[*As the playing goes on* DAVID *suddenly howls like a dog and*
*starts tearing up a hymn-book.*

PETER [*the playing over*]. It's the universal language, Dave. It's
music.

DAVID. Music my universal aunt. It's torture.
[*He finds himself with a page or two of the hymn-book in his*
*hand.*
Here, I know this one.
[*Sings.*] 'All things bright and beautiful——'

PETER [*coming down from the loft*]. That doesn't mean you, Davy.
Put it down.

B                    [ 1 ]

DAVID. 'All creatures great and small—'
  Well, one of those is me: I couldn't miss it.
  'All things wise and wonderful——'

      [CORPORAL JOE ADAMS *comes to the steps with more straw.*

ADAMS. Come and get it!

PETER.                 What is it? Soup?

ADAMS.                     Straw.

PETER. Never could digest it.

      [TIM MEADOWS, *a middle-aged man—indeed he looks well*
  *on towards sixty—limps up to the pile of straw.*

ADAMS. How's the leg feel, Meadows?

MEADOWS.              Ah, all right.
  I wouldn't be heard saying anything about one leg
  I wouldn't say about the other.

PETER.              Where
  Did you get it, chum?

MEADOWS.      I had it for my birthday.
  Quite nice, isn't it? Five toes, it's got.

PETER. I mean where was the fighting, you wit?

MEADOWS [*jerking his head*].       Down the road.
  My Uncle George had a thumping wooden leg,
  Had it with him, on and off, for years.
  When he gave up the world, it got out in the wash house.

DAVID. Has anybody thought what it's going to be like
  Suppose we stay here for months or years?

ADAMS. Best they can do. You heard the towzer Commandant:
  'All more buildings blow up into sky.
  No place like home now. Roof here. Good and kind
  To prisoners. Keep off sun, keep off rain.'

[ 2 ]

PETER. Keep off the grass.

DAVID. It's a festering idea for a prison camp.
You have to think twice every time you think,
In case what you think's a bit on the dubious side.
It's all this smell of cooped-up angels
Worries me.

PETER.          What, us?

DAVID.                    Not mother's angels,
Dumb-cluck, God's angels.

PETER.                    Oh yes, them.
We're a worse fug to them, I shouldn't wonder.
We shall just have to make allowances.

DAVID.                              Beg pardon:
I'm talking to no-complaints Pete: arrangements perfect.

ADAMS. Too many pricking thistles in this straw:
Pricked to hell.

                    [PETER *has wandered across to the lectern.*

PETER.          Note his early perpendicular
Language. Ecclesiastical influence.
See this? They've put us an English Bible.
There's careful nannies for you . . . 'These were the sons
Of Caleb the son of Hur, the firstborn of Ephratah:
Shobal the father of Kirjath-jearim, Salma
The father of Beth-lehem, Hareph the father
Of Beth-gader. And Shobal the father of Kirjath-
Jearim had sons: Haroeh, and half of the Manahethites——'
Interesting, isn't it?

DAVID.                    Stuff it, Pete.

PETER. 'And these were the sons of David, which were born unto
Him in Hebron: the firstborn Amnon, of Ahinoam the

Jezreelitess: the second Daniel, of Abigail the
Carmelitess: the third Absalom the son of Maacah the
Daughter of Talmai king of Geshur: the fourth Adonijah
The son of Haggith: the fifth Shephatiah of Abital:
The sixth Ithream by Eglah his wife . . .'

                                    *Doing*

All right, aren't you, Davey?

DAVID. So I did in Sunday school. You know what Absalom
    Said to the tree? 'You're getting in my hair.'
    And that's what I mean, so shut up.

PETER.                                    Shut up we are.
    Don't mind me. I'm making myself at home.
    Now all I've got to do is try the pulpit.

ADAMS. Watch yourself, Pete. We've got years of this.

DAVID [*his temper growing*]. Any damn where he makes himself at
    home.
    The world blows up, there's Pete there in the festering
    Bomb-hole making cups of tea. I've had it
    Week after week till I'm sick. Don't let's mind
    What happens to anybody, don't let's object to anything,
    Let's give the dirty towzers a cigarette,
    There's nothing on earth worth getting warmed up about!
    It doesn't matter who's on top, make yourself at home.

ADAMS. Character of Private Peter Able:
    And not so far out at that. What we're in for
    We've got to be in for and know just what it is.
    Have some common sense, Pete. If you're looking for trouble
    Go and have it in the vestry.

PETER [*up in the pulpit*]. How can I help it if I can't work myself up
    About the way things go? It's a mystery to me.
    We've had all this before. For God's sake

                        [ 4 ]

Be reasonable, Dave. Perhaps I was meant
To be a bishop.
[*He turns to the nave.*] Dearly beloved brothers
In a general muck-up, towzers included . . .

DAVID. What the hell do you think we're stuck here for
Locked in like lunatics? Just for a nice
New experience, with nice new friends
With nice new rifles to look after us?
We're at war with them, aren't we? And if we are
They're no blaming use!

PETER [*continuing to preach*]. We have here on my left
An example of the bestial passions that beset mankind.

> [DAVID, *beside himself, leaps up the steps and attacks* PETER
> *in the pulpit.*

Davey, Dave . . . don't be a lunatic!

ADAMS.                               Come out of it,
King. Come down here, you great tomfool!

> [*He goes to drag* DAVID *away.* DAVID *has his hands on*
> PETER's *throat and has pushed him across the edge of the*
> *pulpit.*

DAVID [*raging*]. You laugh: I'll see you never laugh again.
Go on: laugh at this.

MEADOWS.             If you don't get your hands away
You'll wish you never had 'em. Give over! Give over!

> [DAVID *releases his hold. He pushes past* ADAMS *and comes*
> *down from the pulpit.*

I see the world in you very well. 'Tisn't
Your meaning, but you're a clumsy, wall-eyed bulldozer.
You don't know what you're hitting.

> [DAVID *goes past him without a word, and throws himself on*
> *to his bed.*

[5]

Ah, well,
Neither do I, of course, come to that.

ADAMS. All right, Peter?

PETER.                              Think so, Corporal,
I'm not properly reassembled yet.
There's a bit of a rattle, but I think I had that before.

ADAMS. Dave had better damp down that filthy volcano
Or let me know what.

PETER.                              Oh, lord, I don't know,
It's who we happen to be. I suppose I'd better
Hit him back some time, or else he'll go mad
Trying to make me see daylight. I don't know.
I'll tell you my difficulty, Corp. I never remember
I ought to be fighting until I'm practically dead.
Sort of absent-fisted. Very worrying for Dave.

[*They have come down from the pulpit.* PETER *sways on his feet.* ADAMS *supports him.*

ADAMS. You're all in, Pete.

PETER.                              Say 'Fall out' and watch me
Fall.

ADAMS. All right, come on, we'll put you to bed.

[MEADOWS *has limped across with two blankets for* PETER's *bunk.* DAVID *is watching anxiously.*

DAVID. What's wrong, Pete?

ADAMS.                              The best thing for you is keep
Out of this.

PETER.         Dog-tired, that's all. It comes
Of taking orders. Dog collar too tight.

[6]

DAVID. I'll see to him.

ADAMS.                    I've seen you see to him.
 Get back on your bed.

DAVID.                    I've never killed him yet.
 I'm a pal of his.

ADAMS.          That's right. I couldn't have expressed it
 Better myself. We'll talk about that tomorrow.

> [*He goes over to make up his own bunk.* DAVID *unlaces*
> PETER'*s boots.*

DAVID. How d'you feel now, Pete?

PETER.                    Beautiful.

DAVID.                              Why don't
 You do some slaughtering sometimes? Why always
 Leave it to me? Got no blood you can heat
 Up or something? I didn't hurt you, did I,
 Pete? How d'you feel?

PETER [*almost asleep*]. Um? Fine.

DAVID [*taking off* PETER'*s socks for him*]. The world's got to have
    us. Things go wrong.
 We've got to finish the dirty towzers. It's been
 A festering day, and I'm stinking tired. See you
 Tomorrow.

> [*He leaves* PETER *sleeping, goes over to his own bunk, and
> throws himself down.*

ADAMS [*to* MEADOWS]. I sometimes feel a bit like Dave
 Myself, about Pete. You have to tell him there's a war on.

> [MEADOWS *has taken his boots and socks off and is lying on
> top of his blankets.*

[7]

MEADOWS. Sometimes I think if it wasn't for the words, Corporal,
   I should be very given to talking. There's things
   To be said which would surprise us if ever we said them.

ADAMS. Don't give us any more surprises, for God's sake.

MEADOWS. There's things would surprise us.

ADAMS [*studying the sole of his foot*]. Like the size of that blister.

MEADOWS. Or even bigger. Well, good night, Corporal.

ADAMS. G'night, boy.

MEADOWS.                I'm old enough to be
   Your father.

ADAMS.          I thought you might be. How did you get
   Pulled in on this?

MEADOWS.             I thought I would.
   I got in under the fence. Not a soul
   At the War Office had noticed me being born.
   I'd only my mother's word for it myself,
   And she never knew whether it was Monday washing-day
   Or Thursday baking-day. She only knew
   I made it hindering awkward.

ADAMS.                          Are you glad
   You came?

MEADOWS. Ah, now. Well,
   Glad, yes, and sorry, yes, and so as that.
   I remember how it came over me, as I
   Was dunging a marrow bed. Tim, I said to me—
   'Cos being a widower I do the old lady's
   Talking for her, since she fell silent—Tim,
   You're in the way to curse. Thinking of the enemy
   And so as that. And I cursed up and about.
   But cursing never made anything for a man yet.

[ 8 ]

So having had the pleasure of it, I came along
To take a hand. But there's strange divisions in us,
And in every man, one side or the other.
When I'm not too good I hear myself talking away
Like Tim Meadows M.P., at the other end of my head.
Sounds all right. I'd like to know what I say.
Might be interesting.

ADAMS.                    I shouldn't worry.
I'm going to take a last look at Pete.
G'night, boy.

MEADOWS [*already almost asleep*].  Hope so.

[ADAMS *goes over to* PETER's *bunk.*

DAVID.                              Corp.

ADAMS.  Hullo.

DAVID.          How long are we here for?

ADAMS.                        A million years.
So you'd better get to like it.

DAVID.              Give us
Cassock and surplice drill tomorrow, Joe.

ADAMS.  O.K. Wash your feet.

DAVID.                How's Pete? Asleep?

ADAMS.  Couldn't be more if he died.

DAVID [*starting up on his elbow*].    What do you mean?

ADAMS.  I mean he's breathing like an easy conscience. Why don't
    you
Get down to it yourself? There's tomorrow to come,
According to orders. Good night, King of Israel.

[9]

DAVID.                                                  Oh, go
And discard yourself. G'night, Corporal Joseph Adams.

> [ADAMS *goes to his bunk.* MEADOWS *turns in his sleep. Th*
> *church clock strikes a single note.*

MEADOWS [*asleep*]. Who's that, fallen out? How many men?
How many? I said only one.
One was enough.
No, no, no. I didn't ask to be God.
No one else prepared to spell the words.
Spellbound. B-o-u-n-d. Ah-h-h-h . . .

> [*He turns in his sleep again*

It's old Adam, old, old, old Adam.
Out of bounds. No one said fall out.
What time did you go to bad?
Sorrow, Adam, stremely sorrow.

> [CORPORAL ADAMS *comes towards him, a dream figure*

Adam, Adam, stand easy there.

ADAMS. Reporting for duty, sir.

MEADOWS. As you were, Adam.

ADAMS. No chance of that, sir.

MEADOWS. As you were, as you were.

ADAMS. Lost all track of it now, sir.

MEADOWS. How far back was it, Adam?

ADAMS [*with a jerk of the head*]. Down the road. Too dark to see.

MEADOWS. Were you alone?

ADAMS.                        A woman with me, sir.

MEADOWS. I said Let there be love,
And there wasn't enough light, you say?

ADAMS. We could see our own shapes, near enough,
   But not the road. The road kept on dividing
   Every yard or so. Makes it long.
   We expected nothing like it, sir.
   Ill-equipped, naked as the day,
   It was all over and the world was on us
   Before we had time to take cover.

MEADOWS. Stand at peace, Adam: do stand at peace.

ADAMS. There's nothing of that now, sir.

MEADOWS. Corporal Adam.

ADAMS.                    Sir?

MEADOWS.                         You have shown spirit.

ADAMS. Thank you, sir.
   Excuse me, sir, but there's some talk of a future.
   I've had no instructions.

MEADOWS [*turning in his sleep*]. Ah-h-h-h-h.

ADAMS. Is there any immediate anxiety of that?

         [DAVID, *as the dream figure of Cain, stands leaning on the
         lectern, chewing at a beet.*

   How far can we fall back, sir?

DAVID [*smearing his arms with beet juice*]. Have you lost something?

ADAMS. Yes, Cain: yes, I have.

DAVID. Have you felt in all your pockets?

ADAMS. Yes, and by searchlight all along the grass
   For God knows howling. Not a sign,
   Not a sign, boy, not a ghost.

DAVID.                         When do you last
   Remember losing it?

ADAMS.                When I knew it was mine.
As soon as I knew it was mine I felt
I was the only one who didn't know
The host.

DAVID.        Poor overlooked
Old man. Allow me to make the introduction.
God: man. Man: God.

> [PETER, *the dream figure of Abel, is in the organ-loft finger*
> *ing out 'Now the day is over'.*

ADAMS. I wish it could be so easy.

DAVID. Sigh, sigh, sigh!
The hot sun won't bring you out again
If you don't know how to behave.
Pretty much like mutiny. I'd like to remind you
We're first of all men, and complain afterwards.
[*Calling.*] Abel! Abel! Hey, flock-headed Peter,
Come down off those mountains.
Those bleating sheep can look after themselves.
Come on down.

PETER.              What for?

DAVID.                    Because I said so!

PETER [*coming down*].  I overlooked the time. Is it day or night?

DAVID. You don't deserve to inherit the earth.
Am I supposed to carry the place alone?

PETER. Where will you carry it?
Where do you think you're going to take it to,
This prolific indifference?
Show me an ending great enough
To hold the passion of this beginning
And raise me to it.

[ 12 ]

Day and night, the sun and moon
Spirit us, we wonder where. Meanwhile
Here we are, we lean on our lives
Expecting purpose to keep her date,
Get cold waiting, watch the overworlds
Come and go, question the need to stay
But do, in an obstinate anticipation of love.
Ah, love me, it's a long misuse of breath
For boys like us. When do we start?

DAVID. When you suffering god'sbodies
Come to your senses. What you'll do
Is lose us life altogether.
Amply the animal is Cain, thank God,
As he was meant to be: a huskular strapling
With all his passions about him. Tomorrow
Will know him well. Momentous doings
Over the hill for the earth and us.
What hell else do you want?

PETER.                    The justification.

DAVID. Oh, bulls and bears to that.
The word's too long to be lived.
Just if, just if, is as far as ever you'll see.

PETER. What's man to be?

DAVID.                    Content and full.

PETER. That's modest enough.
What an occupation for eternity.
Sky's hollow filled as far as for ever
With rolling light: place without limit,
Time without pity:
And did you say all for the sake of our good condition,
All for our two-footed prosperity?

Well, we should prosper, considering
The torment squandered on our prospering.
From squid to eagle the ravening is on.
We are all pain-fellows, but nothing you dismay,
Man is to prosper. Other lives, forbear
To blame me, great and small forgive me
If to your various agonies
My light should seem hardly enough
To be the cause of the ponderable shadow.

DAVID. Who do you think you are, so Angel-sick?
Pain warns us to be master: pain prefers us.
Draws us up.

PETER.          Water into the sun:
All the brooding clouds of us!

DAVID.                              All right.
We'll put it to the High and Mighty.
Play you dice to know who's favoured.

PETER. What's he to do with winning?

DAVID.                              Play you dice.
Not so sure of yourself, I notice.

PETER. I'll play you. Throw for first throw.
Now creation be true to creatures.

ADAMS. Look, sir, my sons are playing.
How silent the spectators are,
World, air, and water.
Eyes bright, tension, halt.
Still as a bone from here to the sea.

DAVID [*playing*]. Ah-h-h-h!

DAMS. Sir, my sons are playing. Cain's your man.
He goes in the mould of passion as you made him.
He can walk this broken world as easily
As I and Eve the ivory light of Eden.
I recommend him. The other boy
Frets for what never came his way,
Will never reconcile us to our exile.
Look, sir, my sons are playing.
Sir, let the future plume itself, not suffer.

ETER [*playing*]. How's that for a nest of singing birds?

DAMS. Cain sweats: Cain gleams. Now do you see him?
He gives his body to the game.
Sir, he's your own making, and has no complaints.

AVID. Ah! What are you doing to me, heaven and earth?

ETER. Friendly morning.

AVID [*shaking the dice*]. Numbers, be true to nature.
                    Deal me high,
                    Six dark stars
                    Come into my sky.

                                        [*He throws.*

Blight! What's blinding me
By twos and threes? I'm strong, aren't I?
Who's holding me down? Who's frozen my fist
So it can't hatch the damn dice out?

ETER [*shaking and throwing*].
                    Deal me high, deal me low.
                    Make my deeds
                    My nameless needs.
                    I know I do not know.
. . . That brings me home!

                [DAVID *roars with rage and disappointment.*

[ 15 ]

DAVID.  Life is a hypocrite if I can't live
    The way it moves me! I was trusted
    Into breath. Why am I doubted now?
    Flesh is my birthplace. Why shouldn't I speak the tongue?
    What's the disguise, eh? Who's the lurcher
    First enjoys us, then disowns us?
    Keep me clean of God, creation's crooked.

ADAMS.  Cain, steady, steady, you'll raise the world.

DAVID.  You bet your roots I will.
    I'll know what game of hide and seek this is.
    Half and half, my petering brother says,
    Nothing of either, in and out the limbo.
    'I know I do not know' he says.
    So any lion can BE, and any ass,
    And any cockatoo: and all the unbiddable
    Roaming voices up and down
    Can live their lives and welcome
    While I go pestered and wondering down hill
    Like a half-wit angel strapped to the back of a mule.
    Thanks! I'll be as the body was first presumed.

PETER.  It was a game between us, Cain.

DAVID [*in a fury*].  Your dice were weighted! You thought yo
    could trick
    The life out of me. We'll see about that.
    You think you're better than you're created!
    I saw the smiles that went between
    You and the top air. I knew your game.
    Look helpless, let him see you're lost,
    Make him amiable to think
    He made more strangely than he thought he did!
    Get out of time, will you, get out of time!
         [*He takes* PETER *by the throat.* ADAMS *goes to part them*

[ 16 ]

ADAMS. Cain, drop those hands!

> [*He is wheeled by an unknown force back against his bunk.*

O Sir,

Let me come to them. They're both
Out of my reach. I have to separate them.

DAVID [*strangling* PETER]. You leave us now, leave us, you half-
and-half:
I want to be free of you!

PETER.                  Cain! Cain!

ADAMS. Cain, Cain!

DAVID.            If life's not good enough for you
Go and justify yourself!

ADAMS. Pinioned here, when out of my body
I made them both, the fury and the suffering,
The fury, the suffering, the two ways
Which here spreadeagle me.

> [DAVID *has fought* PETER *back to the bed and kills him.*

O, O, O,
Eve, what love there was between us. Eve,
What gentle thing, a son, so harmless,
Can hang the world with blood.

DAVID [*to* PETER].            Oh,
You trouble me. You are dead.

ADAMS. How ceaseless the earth is. How it goes on.
Nothing has happened except silence where sound was,
Stillness where movement was. Nothing has happened,
But the future is like a great pit.
My heart breaks, quiet as petals falling
One by one, but this is the drift
Of agony for ever.

C                         [ 17 ]

DAVID.                 Now let's hope
    There will be no more argument,
    No more half-and-half, no more doubt,
    No more betrayal.—You trouble me,
    You trouble me.

MEADOWS [*in his sleep*]. Cain.

                              [DAVID *hides*

                              Cain. Where is
    Your brother?

DAVID.            How should I know? Am I
    His keeper?

ADAMS.         Where is keeping?
    Keep somewhere, world, the time we love.
    I have two sons, and where is one,
    And where will now the other be?
    I am a father unequipped to save.
    When I was young the trees of love forgave me:
    That was all. But now they say
    The days of such simple forgiveness are done,
    Old Joe Adam all sin and bone.

MEADOWS. Cain: I hear your brother's blood
    Crying to me from the ground.

DAVID. Sir, no: he is silent.
    All the crying is mine.

MEADOWS. Run, run, run. Cain
    Is after you.

DAVID.         What shall I do?

MEADOWS. What you have done. It does it to you.
    Nowhere rest. Cage of the world
    Holds your prowling. Howl, Cain, jackal afraid.

And nowhere, Cain, nowhere
Escape the fear of what men fear in you.
Every man's hand will be against you,
But never touch you into quietness.
Run! Run!

VID.        The punishment
Is more than I can bear. I loved life
With a good rage you gave me. And how much better
Did Abel do? He set up his heart
Against your government of flesh.
How was I expected to guess
That what I am you didn't want?
God the jailer, God the gun
Watches me exercise in the yard,
And all good neighbourhood has gone.
The two-faced beater makes me fly,
Fair game, poor game, damned game
For God and all man-hunters.

ADOWS. They shall never kill you.

VID. Death was a big word, and now it has come
An act so small, my enemies will do it
Between two jobs. Cain's alive,
Cain's dead, we'll carry the bottom field:
Killing is light work, and Cain is easily dead.

ADOWS. Run on, keep your head down, cross at the double
The bursts of open day between the nights.
My word is Bring him in alive.
Can you feel it carved on your body?

[DAVID *twists as though he felt a branding iron touch him.*

VID. God in heaven! The drag!
You're tearing me out of my life still living!

[ 19 ]

This can't last on flesh for ever.
Let me sleep, let me, let me, let me sleep.
God, let me sleep. God, let me sleep.

[*He goes into the shadows to his b*

MEADOWS [*turning in bed*]. This can't last on flesh for ever.
Let me sleep.

[*There follows a pause of heavy breathing. The church cl
in the tower strikes the three-quarters.* MEADOWS *wak
props himself up on his elbow.*

Any of you boys awake?
Takes a bit of getting used to, sleeping
In a looming great church. How you doing?
I can't rest easy for the night of me.
. . . Sleeping like great roots, every Jack of them.
How many draughts are sifting under the doors.
Pwhee-ooo. And the breathing: and breathing: heavy and dee
Breathing: heavy and deep.
Sighing the life out of you. All the night.

[DAVID *stirs uneasily.*

DAVID. I don't have to stay here! I'm a King.

MEADOWS. David, that you? You awake, David?
A dream's dreaming him. This is no place
For lying awake. When other men are asleep
A waking man's a lost one. Tim, go byes.

[*He covers his head with his blank

DAVID [*in his sleep*]. I'm King of Israel. They told me so.
I'm doing all right. But who is there to trust?
There are so many fools. Fools and fools and fools,
All round my throne. Loved and alone
David keeps the earth. And nothing kills them.

[ 20 ]

[PETER, *as the dream figure of Absalom, stands with his back pressed against a wall as though afraid to be seen.*

TER. Do you think I care?

VID.                                    Who is that man down there
In the dark alley-way making mischief?

TER. Do you think I care?

VID.                                    Corporal Joab:
There's a man in the dark way. Do you see
That shadow shift? it has a belly and ribs.
It's a man, Joab, who shadows me. He lurks
Against my evening temper. Dangerous.

            [ADAMS *appears as the dream figure of Joab.*

AMS. I think you know already.

VID. He has got to be named. Which of us does it?

AMS. He's your own son: Absalom.

VID.                                    Now
The nightmare sits and eats with me.
He was boy enough.
Why does he look like a thief?

AMS.                                    Because
He steals your good, he steals your strength,
He riddles your world until it sinks,
He plays away all your security,
All you labour and suffer to hold
Against the enemy.

VID.                        The world's back
Is bent and heavily burdened, and yet he thinks
He can leapfrog over. Absalom,
Absalom, why do you play the fool against me?

[ 21 ]

PETER. You and your enemies! Everlastingly
  Thinking of enemies. Open up.
  Your enemies are friends of mine.

DAVID. They gather against our safety. They make trash
  Of what is precious to us. Absalom,
  Come over here. I want to speak to you.

PETER [*running up into the pulpit*]. Do you think I care?

ADAMS.                                    If you let him r
  He'll make disaster certain.

DAVID.                          Absalom,
  Come alive. Living is caring.
  Hell is making straight towards us.

PETER [*in the pulpit*]. Beloved, all who pipe your breath
  Under the salted almond moon,
  Hell is in my father's head
  Making straight towards him. Please forget it.
  He sees the scarlet shoots of spring
  And thinks of blood. He sees the air
  Streaming with imagined hordes
  And conjures them to come. But you and I
  Know that we can turn away
  And everything will turn
  Into itself again. What is
  A little evil here and there between friends?
  Shake hands on it: shake hands, shake hands:
  Have a cigarette, and make yourselves at home.
  Shall we say what we think of the King of Israel?
  Ha—ha—ha!

            [*Jeering laughter echoes round the roof of the chur*

DAVID. Don't do it to me, don't make the black rage
Shake me, Peter. I tremble like an earthquake
Because I can't find words which might
Put the fear of man into you.
Understand! The indecisions
Have to be decided. Who's against us
Reeks to God. Where's your hand?
Be ordinary human, Absalom.

ADAMS. Appeal's no use, King. He has
A foiling heart: the sharp world glances off
And so he's dangerous.

DAVID.                    I think so too.
Who can put eyes in his head? Who'll do it,
Eh, Joab? We have to show him
This terse world means business, don't we, Corporal,
Don't we?

ADAMS.        He has to be instructed.

DAVID. Make a soldier of him. Make him fit
For conflict, as the stars and stags are.
He belongs to no element now. We have
To have him with us. Show him the way,
Joe Adams.

> [PETER *is lounging at the foot of the pulpit.* ADAMS *turns
> to him.*

ADAMS.        Get on parade

PETER.                        What's the music?

ADAMS. I'll sing you, Absalom, if you don't get moving.
And I'll see you singing where you never meant.
Square up.

[ 23 ]

PETER.    What's this?

ADAMS.                Square up, I said.

PETER. Where do we go from here?

ADAMS.                    It's unarmed combat.
  It's how your bare body makes them die.
  It's old hey-presto death: you learn the trick
  And death's the rabbit out of the hat:
  Rolling oblivion for someone.
  You've got to know how to get rid of the rats of the world.
  They're up at your throat. Come on.

PETER. What nightmare's this you're dragging me into?

ADAMS. Humanity's. Come on.

PETER.                    I know
  Nothing about it. Life's all right to me.

ADAMS. Say that when it comes.

                [*The unarmed combat,* ADAMS *instructing*

DAVID. Where is he going now? He carries
  No light with him. Does he know
  The river's unbound: it's up above
  Every known flood-mark, and still rising.

PETER [*who has got away from* ADAMS]. I'm on the other side of the
    river
  Staying with friends, whoever they are.
  Showery still, but I manage to get out,
  I manage to get out.
  The window marked with a cross is where I sleep.
  Just off to a picnic with your enemies.
  They're not bad fellows, once you get to know them.

DAVID [*to* ADAMS]. I have heard from my son.

ADAMS.                        What's his news?

[ 24 ]

DAVID. He's with the enemy. He betrays us, Joab.
He has to be counted with them.
Are we ready?

ADAMS.              Only waiting for the word.

DAVID. We attack at noon.

ADAMS.                  Only hoping for the time.
Good luck.

DAVID.        Good luck.

[ADAMS *walks down the chancel steps and crouches, keeping a steady eye on his wrist-watch.* ADAMS *gives a piercing whistle.* PETER *leaps up and hangs on to the edge of the pulpit.* ADAMS *cuts him down with a tommy-gun. He cries out.* DAVID *starts up in his bunk.* PETER *and* ADAMS *fall to the floor and lie prone.*

[*Awake.*] What's the matter, Peter? Pete! Anything wrong?

[*He gets out of his bunk and goes across to Peter's.*

Pete, are you awake?

[*He stands for a moment and then recrosses the floor.*

MEADOWS [*awake*].      Anything the matter?
Can't you sleep either?

DAVID [*getting back into his bunk*]. I thought I heard
Somebody shout. It woke me up.

MEADOWS.                  Nobody shouted.
I've been lying awake. It's just gone midnight.
There's a howling wind outside plays ducks and drakes
With a flat moon: just see it through this window:
It flips across the clouds and then goes under:
I wish I could run my head against some sleep.

[ 25 ]

This building's big for lying with your eyes open.
You could brush me off, and only think you're dusting.
Who's got the key of the crypt? [*He yawns.*]
Thanks for waking. It brings the population
Up to two. You're a silent chap. Dave?
Have you gone to sleep again already?
Back into the sea, like a slippery seal.
And here am I, high and dry.

DAVID [*asleep*]. Look, look, look.

MEADOWS.                          Away he goes,
Drifting far out. How much of him is left?
Ah, lord, man, go to sleep: stop worrying.

[ADAMS *drags or carries* PETER *to Peter's bunk.*

DAVID. Joab, is that you? Joab, is that you?
What are you bringing back?

ADAMS.                          The victory.

DAVID. Are you sure it is the victory, Joab?
Are we ever sure it's the victory?
So many times you've come back, Joab,
With something else. I want to be sure at last.
I want to know what you mean by victory.
Is it something else to me? Where are you looking?
There's nothing that way. But look over here:
There's something. Along the road, starting the dust,
He wants to reach us. Why is that?
So you're going to walk away.

ADAMS [*going to his bunk*]. I've done my best.
I can't be held responsible for everything.

DAVID. Don't leave me, Joab. Stay and listen.

[ 26 ]

ADAMS [*covering himself over*].          I'm dead beat.
  The enemy's put to flight. Good night, you King of Israel.

DAVID. Bathed in sweat, white with dust. Call him here.
  Come up. I am the King.
  I shall wait patiently until your voice
  Gets back the breath to hit me. I'm here, waiting.

> [DAVID *sits on the edge of his bunk, a red army blanket
> hanging from his shoulder.*

MEADOWS [*awake*]. Where are you off to, Davey?
  Get you back to bed. A dream
  Has got you prisoner, Davey, like
  The world has got us all. Don't let it
  Take you in.

DAVID.          Come here to me, come over
  Here, the dusty fellow with the news,
  Come here. Is the fighting over? Unconditionally?

> [MEADOWS *has left his bunk and crossed to* DAVID.

MEADOWS. Lie down, boy. Forget it. It's all over.

DAVID. Is the young man Absalom safe?

MEADOWS                          Lie down, Dave.
  Everybody's asleep.

ADAMS [*from his bunk*]. The boy's dead.
  You might as well be told: I say
  The boy's dead.

> [DAVID, *giving a groan, lies back on his bed.*

MEADOWS.          The night's over us.
  Nothing's doing. Except the next day's in us
  And makes a difficult sort of lying-in.
  Here, let's cover you up. Keep the day out of this.
  Find something better to sleep about.

[ 27 ]

Give your living heart a rest. Do you hear me,
Dave, down where you are? If you don't mind,
While I'm here, I'll borrow some of that sleep:
You've got enough for two.

[*He limps back to his bunk, passing* ADAMS, *who wakes.*

ADAMS.                              Hullo, Meadows:
What's worrying you?

MEADOWS.                    Dave was. He couldn't
Let go of the day. He started getting up
And walking in his sleep.

ADAMS.                              All right now?

MEADOWS. Seems running smoother.

ADAMS.                                  Is that him talking?

[PETER *has begun to talk in his sleep.*

MEADOWS. Muttering monkeys love us, it's the other one now:
Peter's at it.

PETER.          Do I have to follow you?

ADAMS. You needn't hear him if you get your ears
Under the blankets. That's where I'm going.
Good-night, boy.

[*He disappears under his blankets.* MEADOWS *climbs into his bunk.*

MEADOWS.            Hope so. It's a choppy crossing
We're having still. No coast of daylight yet for miles.

[*He also disappears from view. A pause.*

PETER [*asleep*]. Why did you call me? I'm contented here:
They say I'm in a prison. Morning comes
To a prison like a nurse:

[ 28 ]

A rustling presence, as though a small breeze came,
And presently a voice. I think
We're going to live. The dark pain has gone,
The relief of daylight
Flows over me, as though beginning is
Beginning. The hills roll in and make their homes,
And gradually unfold the plains. Breath
And light are cool together now.
The earth is all transparent, but too deep
To see down to its bed.

[DAVID, *the dream figure of Abraham, stands beside* PETER.

DAVID. Come with me.

PETER. Where are we going?

DAVID. If necessary
To break our hearts. It's as well for the world.

PETER. There's enough breaking, God knows. We die,
And the great cities come down like avalanches.

DAVID. But men come down like living men.
Time gives the promise of time in every death,
Not of any ceasing. Come with me.
The cities are pitifully concerned.
We need to go to the hill.

PETER. What shall we do?

DAVID. What falls to us.

PETER. Falling from where?

DAVID. From the point of devotion, meaning God.
Carry this wood, Isaac, and this coil
Of rope.

PETER. I'm coming.

[ 29 ]

DAVID. There has to be sacrifice.
I know that. There's nothing so sure.

PETER. You walk so fast. These things are heavy.

DAVID. I know. I carry them too.

PETER. I only want
To look around a bit. There's so much to see.
Ah, peace on earth, I'm a boy for the sights.

DAVID. Don't break my heart. You so
Cling hold of the light. I have to take it
All away.

PETER. Why are you so grave?
There's more light than we can hold. Everything
Grows over with fresh inclination
Every day. You and I are both
Immeasurably living.

> [DAVID *has been walking towards the pulpit.* PETER *still lies
> in bed. He starts to whistle a tune, though the whistling seems
> not to come from his lips but from above him.*

DAVID. What do you whistle for?

PETER. I whistle for myself
And anyone who likes it.

DAVID. Keep close to me.
It may not be for long. Time huddles round us,
A little place to be in. And we're already
Up the heavy hill. The singing birds
Drop down and down to the bed of the trees,
To the hay-silver evening, O
Lying gentleness, a thin veil over
The long scars from the nails of the warring hearts.

Come up, son, and see the world.
God dips his hand in death to wash the wound,
Takes evil to inoculate our lives
Against infectious evil. We'll go on.
I am history's wish and must come true,
And I shall hate so long as hate
Is history, though, God, it drives
My life away like a beaten dog. Here
Is the stone where we have to sacrifice.
Make my heart like it. It still is beating
Unhappily the human time.

PETER. Where is the creature that has to die?
There's nothing here of any life worth taking.
Shall we go down again?

DAVID.                    There is life here.

PETER. A flinching snail, a few unhopeful harebells.
What good can they be?

DAVID.                    What else?

PETER.                              You, father,
And me.

DAVID.    I know you're with me. But very strangely
I stand alone with a knife. For the simple asking.
Noon imperial will no more let me keep you
Than if you were the morning dew. The day
Wears on. Shadows of our history
Steal across the sky. For our better freedom
Which makes us living men: for what will be
The heaven on earth, I have to bind you
With cords, and lay you here on the stone's table.

[ 31 ]

PETER. Are you going to kill me? No! Father!
  I've come only a short way into life
  And I can see great distance waiting.
  The free and evening air
  Swans from hill to hill.
  Surely there's no need for us to be
  The prisoners of the dark? Smile, father.
  Let me go.

DAVID.          Against my heart
  I let you go, for the world's own ends
  I let you go, for God's will
  I let you go, for children's children's joy
  I let you go, my grief obeying.
  The cords bind you against my will
  But you're bound for a better world.
  And I must lay you down to sleep
  For a better waking. Come now.

      [*In mime he picks Isaac up in his arms and lays him across*
      *the front of the pulpit.*

PETER [*in his bunk*].                I'm afraid.
  And how is the earth going to answer, even so?

DAVID. As it will. How can we know?
  But we must do, and the future make amends.

PETER. Use the knife quickly. There are too many
  Thoughts of life coming to the cry.
  God put them down until I go.
  Now, now, suddenly!

DAVID [*the knife raised*]. This
  Cuts down my heart, but bitter events must be.

[ 32 ]

I can't learn to forgive necessity:
God help me to forgive it.

[ADAMS *appears as the dream figure of the Angel.*

ADAMS.                     Hold your arm.
There are new instructions. The knife can drop
Harmless and shining.

DAVID.                     I never thought to know,
Strange voice of mercy, such happy descending.
Nor my son again. But he's here untouched,
And evening is at hand
As clear and still as no man.

PETER.                     Father, I feel
The air go over me as though I should live.

DAVID.  So you will, for the earth's while. Shall I
Undo the cords?

ADAMS.                These particular. But never all.
There's no loosening, since men with men
Are like the knotted sea. Lift him down
From the stone to the grass again, and, even so free,
Yet he will find the angry cities hold him.
But let him come back to the strange matter of living
As best he can: and take instead
The ram caught here by the white wool
In the barbed wire of the briar bush:
Make that the kill of the day.

DAVID.                     Readily.

PETER. Between the day and the night
The stars tremble in balance.
The houses are beginning to come to light.
And so it would have been if the knife had killed me.

D

This would have been my death-time.
The ram goes in my place, in a curious changing.
Chance, as fine as a thread,
Cares to keep me, and I go my way.

MEADOWS [*a dream figure*]. Do you want a ride across the sands,
Master Isaac?

PETER.           Who are you?

MEADOWS.                    Now, boy, boy,
Don't make a joke of me. Old Meadows,
The donkey man, who brought you up the hill.
Not remember me? That's a man's memory,
Short measure as that. Down a day.
And we've been waiting, Edwina and me,
As patient as two stale loaves, to take you down.

PETER. But I climbed the hill on foot.

MEADOWS [*patting the bunk*]. No credit, Edwina girl, no credit.
He thinks you're a mangy old moke. You tell him
There's none so mangy as thinks that others are.
You have it for the sake of the world.

PETER. All right, she can take me down. I'm rasping tired.
My whole body's like a three days' growth of beard.
But I don't know why she should have to carry me.
She's nothing herself but two swimming eyes
And a cask of ribs.

MEADOWS.           A back's a back.
She's as good as gold while she lives,
And after that she's as good as dead. Where else
Would you find such a satisfactory soul?
Gee-up, you old millennium. She's slow,
But it's kind of onwards. Jog, jog,
Jog, jog.

[ 34 ]

PETER.     There's a ram less in the world tonight.
My heart, I could see, was thudding in its eyes.
It was caught, and now it's dead.

MEADOWS.                              Jog, jog,
Jog, jog, jog, jog, jog,
Jog, jog.

PETER. Across the sands and into the sea.
The sun flocks along the waves.
Blowing up for rain of sand.
Helter-shelter.

MEADOWS.     Jog. Jog. Jog.
Donkey ride is over. In under
The salty planks and corrugated iron.
Stable for mangy mokes. Home, old girl,
Home from the sea, old Millie-edwinium.
Tie up here.

                              [*He has climbed into his bunk.*

PETER.          No eyes open. All
In sleep. The innocence has come.
Ram's wool hill pillow is hard.

          [*He sighs and turns in his bunk. The church clock strikes one.
          An aeroplane is heard flying over the church.* PETER *wakens
          and sits up in his bunk, listening.*

Is that one of ours?

MEADOWS [*his face emerging from the blankets*].
                    Just tell me: are you awake
Or asleep?

PETER.     Awake. Listen. Do you hear it?
Is it one of ours?

MEADOWS.              No question: one of ours.
Or one of theirs.

PETER.              Gone over. Funny question:
'Was I asleep?' when I was sitting up
Asking you a question.

MEADOWS.              Dave's been sitting up
Asking questions, as fast asleep as an old dog.
And you've been chatting away like old knitting-needles,
Half the night.

PETER.              What was I saying?

MEADOWS.              I know all
Your secrets now, man.

PETER.              I wish I did.
What did I say?

MEADOWS.              Like the perfect gentleman
I obliterated my lug-holes:
Under two blankets, army issue.
A man must be let to have a soul to himself
Or souls will go the way of tails.
I wouldn't blame a man for sleeping.
It comes to some. To others it doesn't come.
Troubles differ. But I should be glad
To stop lying out here in the open
While you underearthly lads
Are shut away talking night's language like natives.
We only have to have Corporal Adams
To make a start, and I might as well
Give up the whole idea. Oh, lord, let me
Race him to it. I'm going under now
For the third time.

                    [*He covers his head with the blankets.*

PETER.               Sorry if I disturbed you.
   I'll go back where I came from, and if I can
   I'll keep it to myself. Poor old Meadows:
   Try thinking of love, or something.
   Amor vincit insomnia.

MEADOWS.              That's enough
   Of night classes. What's it mean?

PETER. The writing on the wall. So turn
   Your face to it: get snoring.

MEADOWS.                 Not hereabouts:
   It wouldn't be reverent. Good night, then.

PETER.                              Same to you.

   [*They cover their heads. A pause.* ADAMS, *asleep, lies flat
   on his bunk, looking down over the foot of it.*

ADAMS. Fish, fish, fish in the sea, you flash
   Through your clouds of water like the war in heaven:
   Angel-fish and swordfish, the silver troops . . .
   And I am salt and sick on a raft above you,
   Wondering for land, but there's no homeward
   I can see.

                          [*He turns on his back.*
           God, have mercy
   On our sick shoals, darting and dying.
   We're strange fish to you. How long
   Can you drift over our sea, and not give up
   The ghost of hope? The air is bright between us.
   The flying fish make occasional rainbows,
   But land, your land and mine, is nowhere yet.

          [DAVID, *a dream figure, comes to meet him.*

[ 37 ]

How can a man learn navigation
When there's no rudder? You can seem to walk,
You there: you can seem to walk:
But presently you drown.

DAVID.                              Who wants us, Corporal?

ADAMS. I wish I knew. I'm soaked to the skin.
The world shines wet. I think it's men's eyes everywhere
Reflecting light. Presently you drown.

DAVID. Have you forgotten you're a prisoner?
They marched us thirty miles in the pouring rain.
Remember that? They, they, they, they.

> [PETER *comes down towards* DAVID, *marching but ex-*
> *hausted. As he reaches* DAVID *he reels and* DAVID *catches*
> *him.*

PETER. What happens if I fall out, Dave?

DAVID. You don't fall out, that's all.

PETER. They can shoot me if they like.
It'll be a bit of a rest.

DAVID. You're doing all right.

PETER. I wouldn't know. It. Feels.
Damned. Odd. To me.

DAVID.                              Corporal Adams,
Man half-seas overboard!
Can you lend a hand?

ADAMS [*jumping from his bunk*]. Here I come.
Does he want to be the little ghost?
Give us an arm. Dave and I will be
Your anchor, boy: keep you from drifting
Away where you're not wanted yet.

PETER. Don't think you've got me with you.
  I dropped out miles ago.

ADAMS. We'll keep the memory green.

> [*They do not move forward, but seem to be trudging.*

DAVID. They, they, they, they.

ADAMS. Be careful how you step. These logs we're on
  Are slimy and keep moving apart.

DAVID [*breaking away*]. Where do you think we are?
  We're prisoners, God! They've bricked us in.

ADAMS. Who said you were dismissed?

PETER.                              Forget your stripes
  For a minute, Corporal: it's my birthday next month,
  My birthday, Corporal: into the world I came,
  The barest chance it happened to be me,
  The naked truth of all that led the way
  To make me. I'm going for a stroll.

> [*He wanders down towards the lectern.*

ADAMS. Where are you going? Orders are
  No man leaves unless in a state of death.

DAVID. There's nowhere to go, and he knows
  There's nowhere to go. He's trying to pretend
  We needn't be here.

PETER.              Don't throttle yourself
  With swallowing, Dave. Anyone
  Would think you never expected the world.
  Listen to the scriptures:
  [*As though reading the Bible.*]
      Nebuchadnezzar, hitting the news,
      Made every poor soul lick his shoes.

[ 39 ]

When the shoes began to wear
Nebuchadnezzar fell back on prayer.
Here endeth the first lesson. And here beginneth
The second lesson . . .

DAVID.                         I'll read the second lesson:
God drown you for a rat, and let the world
Go down without you.

PETER.   Three blind mice of Gotham,
            Shadrac, Meshac and Abednego:
            They went to walk in a fire.
            If the fire had been hotter
            Their tales would have been shorter.
Here endeth——

ADAMS.  Get into the ranks.

PETER.  What's worrying you? We're not
On active service now. Maybe it's what
They call in our paybooks 'disembodied service':
So drill my spirit, Corporal, till it weeps
For mercy everywhere.

DAVID.                         It had better weep,
It had better weep. By God, I'll say
We have to be more than men if we're to man
This rising day. They've been keeping from us
Who we are, till now, when it's too late
To recollect. [*Indicating* PETER.] Does he know?

ADAMS.  Shadrac, Meshac, Abednego—
We didn't have those names before: I'll swear
We were at sea. This black morning
Christens us with names that were never ours
And makes us pay for them. Named,

Condemned. What they like to call us
Matters more than anything at heart.
Hearts are here to stop
And better if they do. God help us all.

PETER. Do I know what?

ADAMS.                    We are your three blind mice:
Our names are Shadrac, Meshac, and Abednego.
This is our last morning. Who knows truly
What that means, except us?

PETER.                    And which of us
Knows truly? O God in heaven, we're bound
To wake up out of this. Wake, wake, wake:
This is not my world! Where have you brought me?

DAVID. To feed what you've been riding pick-a-back.

PETER. I can believe anything, except
The monster.

DAVID.          And the monster's here.

ADAMS.                              To make
Sure we know eternity's in earnest.

PETER. It's here to kill. What's that in earnest of?
But the world comes up even over the monster's back.
Corporal, can we make a dash for the hill there?

ADAMS. We're under close arrest.

DAVID.                    O God, are we
To be shut up here in what other men do
And watch ourselves be ground and battered
Into their sins? Let me, dear God, be active
And seem to do right, whatever damned result.
Let me have some part in what goes on
Or I shall go mad!

[ 41 ]

PETER.                    What's coming now?
Their eyes are on us. Do you see them?

ADAMS.  Inspection. The powers have come to look us over
To see if we're in fettle for the end.
Get into line.

DAVID.            What, for those devils?
Who are they?

ADAMS.                Nebuchadnezzar and his aides.
Do what you're told.

PETER.                    Is that him with one eye?

DAVID.  Are they ours or theirs?

ADAMS.                        Who are we, Dave, who
Are we? If we could get the hang of that
We might know what side they're on. I should say
On all sides. Which is why the open air
Feels like a barrack square.

PETER.                        Is that him
With one eye?

ADAMS.          If we could know who we are——

DAVID.  I've got to know which side I'm on.
I've got to be on a side.

ADAMS.                    —They're coming up.
Let's see you jump to it this time: we're coming
Up for the jump. We can't help it if
We hate his guts.—Look out.—Party, shun!

                            [*They all come to attention.*

The three prisoners, sir.—Party, stand
At ease!

PETER.    Purple and stars and red and gold.
What are they celebrating?

[ 42 ]

DAVID. We shall know soon.

ADAMS. Stop talking in the ranks.

[*They stand silent for a moment.*

PETER. What bastard language
Is he talking? Are we supposed to guess?
Police on earth. Aggression is the better
Part of Allah. Liberating very high
The dying and the dead. Freedoom, freedoom.
Will he never clear his throat?

DAVID. He's moving on.

ADAMS. Party, at-ten-tion!
[*They bring their heels together, but they cannot bring their
hands from behind their backs.*

PETER. Corporal, our hands are tied!

DAVID. They've played their game
In the dark: we're theirs, whoever calls us.

ADAMS. Stand at ease.

DAVID. Our feet are tied!

PETER. Hobbled,
Poor asses.

ADAMS. That leaves me without a word of command
To cover the situation, except
Fall on your knees.

PETER. What's coming, Corporal?

ADAMS. You two, let's know it: we have to meet the fire.

DAVID. Tied hand and foot: not men at all!

PETER. O how
Shall we think these moments out
Before thinking splits to fear. I begin

[ 43 ]

To feel the sweat of the pain: though the pain
Hasn't reached us yet.

ADAMS.                Have your hearts ready:
It's coming now.

DAVID.             Every damned forest in the world
Has fallen to make it. The glare's on us.

PETER.                    Dead on.
And here's the reconnoitring heat:
It tells us what shall come.

ADAMS.               Now then! Chuck down
Your wishes for the world: there's nothing here
To charm us. Ready?

DAVID.             I've been strong.
The smoke's between us. Where are you, Adams?

ADAMS. Lost.

PETER.        Where are you, Adams?

                       [ADAMS *cries out and falls to his knees.*

DAVID. It's come to him, Peter!

PETER.                We shall know!

DAVID. Scalding God!

             [*They, too, have fallen to their knees.*

ADAMS. What way have I come down, to find
I live still, in this round of blaze?
Here on my knees. And a fire hotter
Than any fire has ever been
Plays over me. And I live. I know
I kneel.

DAVID.     Adams.

ADAMS.         We're not destroyed.

DAVID. Adams.

PETER.                Voices. We're men who speak.

DAVID. We're men who sleep and wake.
   They haven't let us go.

PETER.                My breath
   Parts the fire a little.

ADAMS.                But the cords
   That were tying us are burnt: drop off
   Like snakes of soot.

PETER.                Can we stand?

DAVID. Even against this coursing fire we can.

PETER. Stand: move: as though we were living,
   In this narrow shaking street
   Under the eaves of seven-storeyed flames
   That lean and rear again, and still
   We stand. Can we be living, or only
   Seem to be?

ADAMS.        I can think of life.
   We'll make it yet.

DAVID.                That's my devotion.
   Which way now?

PETER.                Wait a minute. Who's that
   Watching us through the flame?

        [MEADOWS, *a dream figure, is sitting on the side of his bunk.*

DAVID.                Who's there?

ADAMS. Keep your heads down. Might be
   Some sniper of the fire.

                        [MEADOWS *crows like a cock.*

PETER.                A lunatic.

[ 45 ]

ADAMS [*calling to* MEADOWS]. Who are you?

MEADOWS.                              Man.

ADAMS.                                        Under what command?

MEADOWS. God's.

ADAMS.                May we come through?

MEADOWS.                                        If you have
  The patience and the love.

DAVID.                        Under this fire?

MEADOWS. Well, then, the honesty.

ADAMS.                                        What honesty?

MEADOWS. Not to say we do
  A thing for all men's sake when we do it only
  For our own. And quick eyes to see
  Where evil is. While any is our own
  We sound fine words unsoundly.

ADAMS.                                You cockeyed son
  Of heaven, how did you get here?

MEADOWS. Under the fence. I think they forgot
  To throw me in. But there's not a skipping soul
  On the loneliest goat-path who is not
  Hugged into this, the human shambles.
  And whatever happens on the farthest pitch,
  To the sand-man in the desert or the island-man in the sea,
  Concerns us very soon. So you'll forgive me
  If I seem to intrude.

PETER.                        Do you mean to stay here?

MEADOWS. I can't get out alone. Neither can you.

[ 46 ]

But, on the other hand, single moments
Gather towards the striking clock.
Each man is the world.

PETER.                    But great events
Go faster.

DAVID.        Who's to lead us out of this?

MEADOWS.  It's hard to see. Who will trust
What the years have endlessly said?

ADAMS.  There's been a mort of time. You'd think
Something might have come of it. These men
Are ready to go, and so am I.

PETER.  But there's no God-known government anywhere.

MEADOWS.  Behind us lie
The thousand and the thousand and the thousand years
Vexed and terrible. And still we use
The cures which never cure.

DAVID.                    For mortal sake,
Shall we move? Do we just wait and die?

MEADOWS.  Figures of wisdom back in the old sorrows
Hold and wait for ever. We see, admire
But never suffer them: suffer instead
A stubborn aberration.
O God, the fabulous wings unused,
Folded in the heart.

DAVID.                    So help me, in
The stresses of this furnace I can see
To be strong beyond all action is the strength
To have. But how do men and forbearance meet?
A stone forbears when the wheel goes over, but that
Is death to the flesh.

[ 47 ]

ADAMS. And every standing day
  The claims are deeper, inactivity harder.
  But where, in the maze of right and wrong,
  Are we to do what action?

PETER. Look, how intense
  The place is now, with swaying and troubled figures.
  The flames are men: all human. There's no fire!
  Breath and blood chokes and burns us. This
  Surely is unquenchable? It can only transform.
  There's no way out. We can only stay and alter.

DAVID. Who says there's nothing here to hate?

MEADOWS. The deeds, not those who do.

ADAMS. Strange how we trust the powers that ruin
  And not the powers that bless.

DAVID. But good's unguarded,
  As defenceless as a naked man.

MEADOWS. Imperishably. Good has no fear;
  Good is itself, what ever comes.
  It grows, and makes, and bravely
  Persuades, beyond all tilt of wrong:
  Stronger than anger, wiser than strategy,
  Enough to subdue cities and men
  If we believe it with a long courage of truth.

DAVID. Corporal, the crowing son of heaven
  Thinks we can make a morning.

MEADOWS. Not
  By old measures. Expedience and self-preservation
  Can rot as they will. Lord, where we fail as men
  We fail as deeds of time.

[ 48 ]

PETER. The blaze of this fire
  Is wider than any man's imagination.
  It goes beyond any stretch of the heart.

MEADOWS. The human heart can go to the lengths of God.
  Dark and cold we may be, but this
  Is no winter now. The frozen misery
  Of centuries breaks, cracks, begins to move;
  The thunder is the thunder of the floes,
  The thaw, the flood, the upstart Spring.
  Thank God our time is now when wrong
  Comes up to face us everywhere,
  Never to leave us till we take
  The longest stride of soul men ever took.
  Affairs are now soul size.
  The enterprise
  Is exploration into God.
  Where are you making for? It takes
  So many thousand years to wake,
  But will you wake for pity's sake?
  Pete's sake, Dave or one of you,
  Wake up, will you? Go and lie down.
  Where do you think you're going?

ADAMS [*waking where he stands*]. What's wrong?

MEADOWS. You're walking in your sleep.
  So's Pete and Dave. That's too damn many.

ADAMS. Where's this place? How did I get here?

MEADOWS. You were born here, chum. It's the same for all of us.
  Get into bed.

PETER [*waking*]. What am I doing here?

MEADOWS. Walking your heart out, boy.

[ 49 ]

ADAMS.                                    Dave, Dave.

MEADOWS. Let him come to himself gentle but soon
    Before he goes and drowns himself in the font.

ADAMS. Wake up, Dave.

PETER.                     I wish I knew where I was.

MEADOWS. I can only give you a rough idea myself.
    In a sort of a universe and a bit of a fix.
    It's what they call flesh we're in.
    And a fine old dance it is.

DAVID [*awake*].          Did they fetch us up?

MEADOWS. Out of a well. Where Truth was.
    They didn't like us fraternizing. Corp,
    Would you mind getting your men to bed
    And stop them trapsing round the precincts?

ADAMS. Dave, we're mad boys. Sleep gone to our heads.
    Come on.

DAVID.      What's the time?

ADAMS.                     Zero hour.

DAVID. It feels like half an hour below. I've got cold feet.

PETER. [*already lying on his bunk*]   I've never done that before. I
    wonder now
    What gives us a sense of direction in a dream?
    Can we see in sleep? And what would have happened
    If we'd walked into the guard? Would he have shot us,
    Thinking we were trying to get out?

MEADOWS. So you were from what you said. I could stand
    One at a time, but not all three together.

[ 50 ]

It began to feel like the end of the world
With all your bunks giving up their dead.

ADAMS. Well, sleep, I suppose.

DAVID.                              Yeh. God bless.

PETER. Rest you merry.

MEADOWS.              Hope so. Hope so.

> [*They settle down. The church clock strikes. A bugle sounds in the distance.*

### THE PLAY ENDS

PRINTED IN
GREAT BRITAIN
AT THE
UNIVERSITY PRESS
OXFORD
BY
CHARLES BATEY
PRINTER
TO THE
UNIVERSITY